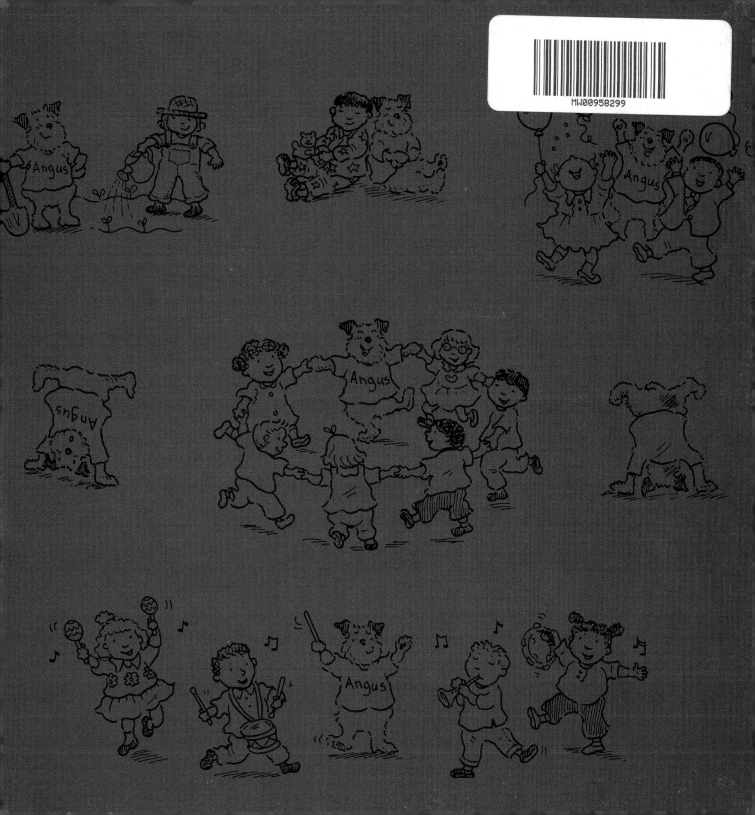

*To all the dentists and hygienists who take care of children
(with very special thanks to Dr. "Ruth the Tooth" Becker
and the American Academy of Pediatric Dentistry)
and always to Erik, Emma, and Wyatt, with love*
—H. M.

*To a very special dentist, Dr. Robert K. Shimasaki,
and his wonderful staff*
—L. R.

What to Expect When You Go to the Dentist
Text and illustrations copyright © 2002 by Heidi Murkoff
What to Expect Kids® is a registered trademark of Heidi Murkoff.
Growing Up Just Got Easier™ and Angus™ are trademarks of Heidi Murkoff.
HarperCollins®, ✿®, and HarperFestival® are registered trademarks of HarperCollins Publishers Inc.
Manufactured in China. All rights reserved.
Library of Congress catalog card number: 99-69937
www.harperchildrens.com

What to Expect
When You Go
to the Dentist

Heidi Murkoff

Illustrated by Laura Rader

HarperFestival®
A Division of HarperCollinsPublishers

A Word to Parents

When you were growing up it was more than likely that the dentist's office wasn't your favorite place to go. If you're like most adults today (who cut their teeth before teeth started being protected by fluoridated water, fluoride treatments, and sealants), you probably associated dental visits with drillings, fillings, and other painful procedures. Chances are you still do.

But a lot has changed in dentistry since you were a kid, especially for children. For one thing, though family dentistry is alive and well, pediatric dentists have become an ideal option for many younger patients. Many dentists who specialize in children seem to have minored in fun and games at dental school. A visit to their colorful, child-friendly, attraction-packed offices is a walk in the park compared to visits to dental offices of the past. For another thing, thanks to improvements in prevention, today's child is far less likely to require drillings and fillings. And thanks to improvements in technology, those who do are likely never to associate dental procedures with pain.

Still, any new or unfamiliar experience triggers a certain amount of trepidation in young children, and a visit to the dentist, especially if it's a first visit, is no exception. That's why positive preparation is so important. Helping your child understand who dentists are, what

they do, and why we go to them for checkups will allow him or her to sit back in the dentist chair, relax, and have fun. It may also encourage your child to become an active participant in his or her own dental health maintenance (brushing and flossing, anyone?), participation that could lead to a much brighter dental future.

What to Expect When You Go to the Dentist is a good place to start preparing for a life of healthy teeth. It will answer many of the questions your child may have about an upcoming dental visit, about dentists in general, and about why taking care of your teeth is so important. It will take your child step-by-step through a checkup, from the waiting room to the fluoride treatment, so that he or she can arrive at the dentist's office knowing exactly what to expect.

Role-playing has a place, too. Pretending to be a dentist—practicing on dolls, stuffed animals, and willing parents—can empower your child, making him or her a less reluctant patient when the time comes. It's also important, especially if you have dental anxiety, to try not to relay to your child any fears you may have about dental visits. The less said about your root canals the better. Also, avoid using a trip to the dentist as a threat ("If you don't brush your teeth, you'll have to go to the dentist!"), or your child could come to equate dental visits with punishment.

Wishing you many happy trips to the dentist's office and a lifetime of happy smiles....

Heidi

Let's visit the dentist and learn how to keep our teeth healthy!

Just Ask Angus

Hello! My name is Angus. Some people call me the Answer Dog, because I like to answer all kinds of questions about growing up. It's good to ask questions because what you know, helps you grow!

So, I hear you're going to the dentist soon. Or maybe you just want to find out more about dentists. Either way, I bet you have lots of questions. I'm going to show you and tell you everything there is to know about dentists: what they do, what their offices are like, and what might happen when you have a checkup at the dentist. That way, when you go to the dentist, you'll know exactly what to expect.

Are you ready to find out what to expect when you go to the dentist? Then let's get started! Follow me....

Your friend,

 Angus

P.S. I've put a little game or idea to think about on the bottom of every page. Look for my paw print, and you'll find it! Have fun!

What's a dentist?

A dentist is a doctor for your teeth. It's a dentist's job to keep people's teeth healthy, just like it's a doctor's job to keep people's bodies healthy. It's hard work keeping people's teeth healthy. That's why dentists have helpers called assistants or hygienists. Some dentists and hygienists only take care of children's teeth, some only take care of grown-ups' teeth, and some take care of children's and grown-ups' teeth. Dentists and hygienists who take care of children's teeth like children a lot, so they try to make going to the dentist as much fun as possible!

Do you like to pretend to be a dentist? It's fun to practice on your dolls or stuffed animals—or even on your mommy and daddy!

You can play dentist with Mommy or Daddy. Use a tiny flashlight to check their teeth.

Why do I have to go to the dentist?

Open your mouth, look in a mirror, and you'll see exactly why you have to go to the dentist. . . . You have teeth! Everybody who has teeth goes to the dentist, because everybody wants to keep their teeth healthy, clean, and strong. Little children go to the dentist, big children go to the dentist, mommies and daddies and teachers go to the dentist.

Keeping teeth healthy is very important, because you need teeth for some very important things. How do you use your teeth?

What does a dentist's office look like?

Just like a doctor's office, a dentist's office has a waiting room and checkup rooms. The waiting room is where you'll stay until it's your turn to see the dentist. It will probably have some toys and books to keep you busy, but it's a good idea to bring something from home, too. (If you bring a special stuffed animal, it can sit on your lap and keep you company while your teeth are being checked.) The checkup room is where the dentist and the hygienist will check and clean your teeth. It will have a big chair for you to sit on. The big chair isn't like anything you have at home. It has a sink attached to it, so you can rinse and spit without getting up. And the whole chair moves up and down and leans all the way back so the dentist can see your teeth better. It's fun to take rides in the dentist chair!

Before you go to the dentist, or while you're waiting in the waiting room, make a picture to give to the dentist. I bet the dentist will love it!

That's great! I bet the dentist will love it!

What happens at the dentist?

Lots of interesting things happen at the dentist's office. Your dentist may explain them all, but don't forget to ask questions, too! The dentist will count your teeth by tapping on each one. (Don't forget to ask how many teeth you have!) She'll also check each tooth to make sure it's strong and healthy and to look for cavities. Healthy teeth are clean teeth! At checkups, the dentist or hygienist may put a special red liquid on your teeth that will make them look like they're painted red (don't worry, it'll come right off when your teeth are cleaned). This shows the dentist where you're doing a good job brushing (where your teeth are not red) and where you need to brush better (where your teeth are very red). Then the dentist or hygienist will give your teeth a super cleaning! At some checkups, your dentist may also take a picture of your teeth called an X ray. Say cheese!

If you don't like bright lights, you can bring sunglasses to the dentist's office. Then while the dentist checks your teeth, you can pretend you're lying on the beach!

You can almost hear the waves!

What will the dentist do with all those tools?

When you visit the dentist, you'll see a lot of interesting tools. There's a tool for scraping away icky old food that's stuck to your teeth and a tool for scooping it up. There's a tool with a mirror at the end, so the dentist can see more clearly behind and between your teeth. There's a tool, like a little hose, that squirts water in your mouth to clean it (I call this Mr. Squirty). Then there's a tool, like a straw, that sucks the extra water out of your mouth (I like to call that Mr. Thirsty). The best tool of all is the special toothbrush. It goes around and around your teeth to make them shinier, brighter, and cleaner than they've ever been before. Not only that—you get to pick out a yummy-flavored toothpaste to use on it! What's your favorite flavor?

Look down and say "ptooey" when you spit.

Angus

One way to help is by learning how to rinse and spit. Have a grown-up help you practice. Fill a cup with water, swish the water around in your mouth, and then spit the water into the sink. Try not to swallow any!

The Dentist's Special Tools for Healthy Teeth
by Angus

Mirror - for a closer view

These tools remove old food! Yuck!

Mr. Thirsty

Mr. Squirty

I ♥ clean teeth!

All these special tools help to keep your teeth clean!

Polishing tool

TOOL BOX

toothpaste

dental floss

toothbrush

Your "tools"

Does a tooth checkup hurt?

ooth checkups don't hurt at all, but some things the dentist does may feel a little different. You'll feel a tickling feeling on your teeth when the toothbrush cleans them, a wet feeling when "Mr. Squirty" sprays water into your mouth, and a sucking feeling when "Mr. Thirsty" sucks up the water. You will also hear some different noises: a scraping sound, a humming sound, a buzzing sound, a gurgling sound, and a vacuum-cleaner sound. Those are the sounds the dentist's tools make when they're busy working to help your teeth stay healthy, clean, and strong!

One of the best ways to help the dentist while you're getting your checkup is to hold very still when he asks you to. Practice in a chair at home (no wiggling!). How long can you sit still?

Let's count how long you can sit still. Get ready. Starting … NOW!

Why does the dentist have to clean my teeth?

Cleaning your teeth helps keep them healthy. Of course, brushing your teeth at home helps, too. But even if you brush your teeth every single day, the dentist or hygienist still needs to give them a super cleaning at your checkups. That's because bits of food can get stuck in between your teeth and in other spaces where your toothbrush may not reach. Food turns into sticky goop called plaque, which can be bad for your teeth if it stays there too long. When the dentist or hygienist scrapes and brushes away that plaque with her special tools, your teeth will be super clean. And that's something to smile about.

When you brush and floss at home, one good way to make sure you get your teeth as clean as can be is to check in the mirror when you're done. Look carefully for little bits of food. . . . They might be hiding!

Open wide and check carefully!

At Home

At the Dentist

What's an X ray?

The dentist can see the outside of your teeth just by looking at them with a bright light and a little mirror. But to see the inside of your teeth and in between them, too, the dentist may need to take pictures called X rays. You won't have to smile to take these pictures, but you will have to open your mouth really wide! You'll also have to wear a special apron and sit very still. (I know you're good at that because you've been practicing!) Your dentist will save all of your X rays, putting them together in a photo album that shows how your teeth change as you grow up. Don't forget to ask your dentist to show you what your teeth look like on the X ray!

Wow! Look at all those teeth!

Opening your mouth really, really wide helps the dentist better check your teeth. Practice at home before you go. Can you open your mouth as wide as a lion or a crocodile?

A Look Inside With X rays

knee

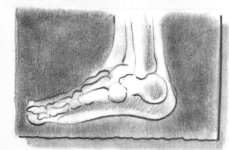

foot

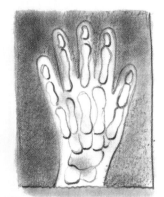

hand

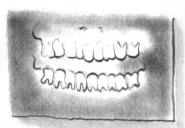

teeth

your lunch box

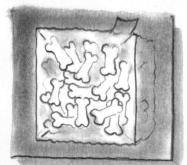

Angus's snack

X rays show what things look like inside!

What's a cavity?

A cavity is a soft spot in your tooth. Sometimes cavities hurt a little, but most of the time they don't hurt at all. Every time you have a checkup, the dentist will check your teeth to see if any of them have a cavity. If one does have a cavity, you'll probably come back for another visit so the dentist can clean out the soft spot and fill it up with a special tooth-fixing coating. The special coating, called a filling, is sort of like a tooth Band-Aid. The filling makes your tooth strong and healthy again.

Brushing your teeth after you eat is the best way to protect your teeth from cavities. But when you're not home and can't brush, there's something else you can do: swish and swallow. That washes away most of the leftover food. Try swishing and swallowing some water now!

Take a drink, swish, and swallow!

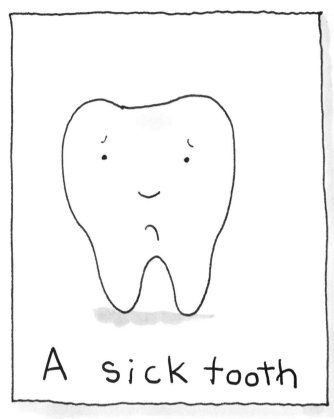

A sick tooth

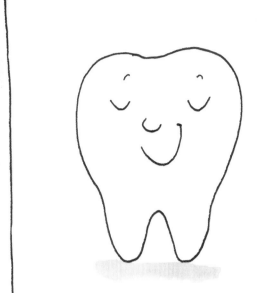

A healthy tooth

A filling can make a sick tooth become healthy again.

How can I help keep my teeth healthy?

There are plenty of ways you can keep your teeth healthy, and your dentist will probably tell you about all of them. One way is to brush your teeth with a grown-up's help at least twice a day, especially after breakfast and before bed. It's also important to floss between your teeth. You'll need a grown-up to help you with that, too! Something else you can do (with no help at all!) is to eat lots of foods that help make your teeth strong—like cheese, yogurt, milk, and fresh fruit and vegetables (especially crunchy ones, like apples and carrots). Not eating sticky foods very often (like candy and fruit snacks), and if you should eat them, always brushing or swishing and swallowing afterward, can also help. And, of course, don't forget to go to the dentist for your cleanings and checkups. After all, no one knows more about how to keep your teeth healthy than your dentist does!

With your mommy or daddy's help, make a healthy-tooth chart for your bathroom. Check off on the chart every time you brush and floss!